HER MAJESTY THE QUEEN ELIZABETH II

By David Chung
Illustrated by Farimah Khavarinezhad

ISBN-13: 978-1-954962-01-9 (hardcover)
ISBN-13: 978-1-954962-00-2 (paperback)

verycoolpress.com

To Mom,
Our Queen.

When Queen Elizabeth was a little girl, she didn't think she was going to be queen at all.

Her Uncle David was the eldest son of King George V and he was going to be the king next.

But when he was made king, he was in love
with a lady who had been divorced twice,

and the British government said that he wasn't allowed to marry a divorced lady, not even if she had only been divorced once.

So King Edward VIII (which was the regal name that Uncle David took to be king) thought about it for a little while,

and then decided he wanted to
be married to the lady more
than he wanted to be king.

And so he abdicated, which is what it is called when a king or queen says they don't want to be king or queen any more.

Daily Mirror

THE KING DECIDES :
ABDICATION PLANS

This meant that Elizabeth's dad was king, and one day, she would become the queen.

She was 26 years old when she became the queen, and was already married to Prince Philip

and they had two children, Prince Charles and Princess Anne.

Prince Charles will be king in time.

The queen was very busy for some years when she was first made queen.

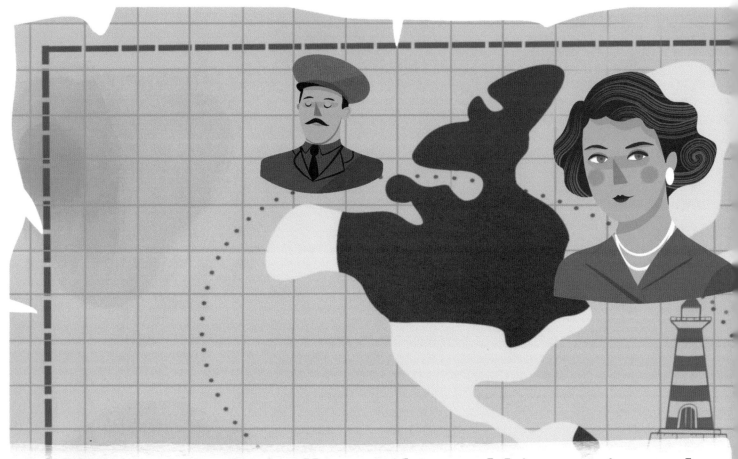

She was traveling all over the world to greet people from countries that used to be colonized by the British (that's when British people went to places and said, "We're going to live here and be in charge!")

who were then in the Commonwealth (which is sort of when the British said, "Oops, that was quite rude of us to colonize you, we want to be friends now").

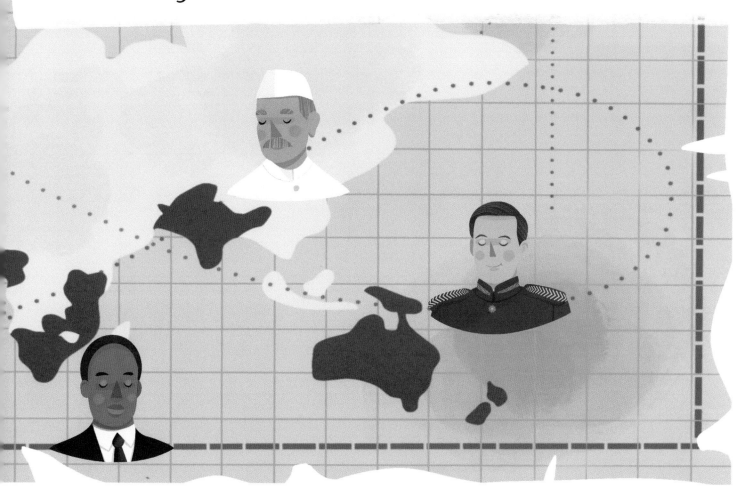

But when the queen had finished traveling all about, she decided to have two more children, and she had Prince Andrew and Prince Edward.

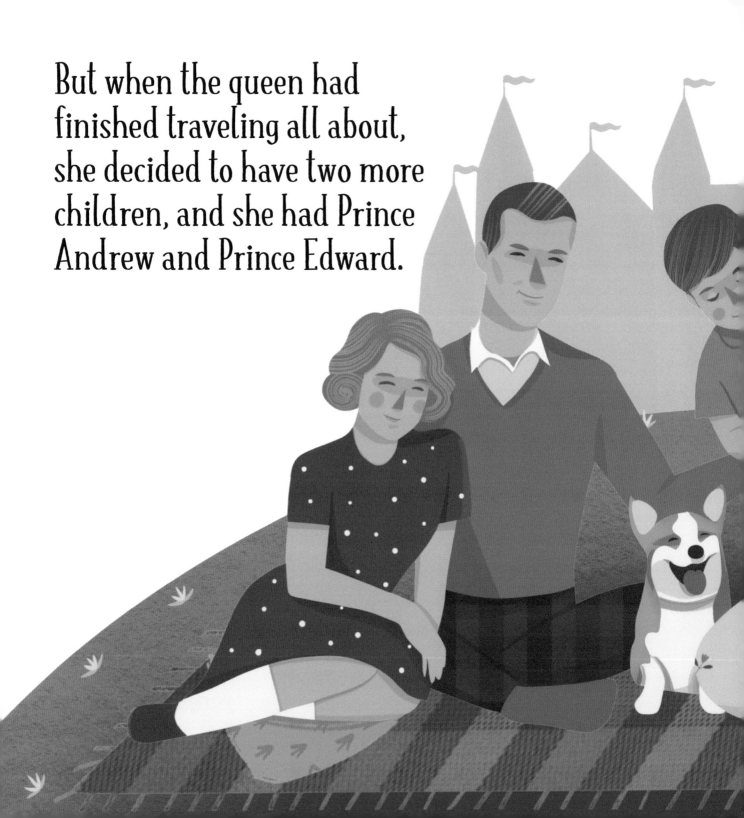

With four children, lots of dogs and plenty of horses, the queen was happy with her family — and still very much in love with Prince Philip

He is not called king, because she is the monarch. Instead, he is a Prince Consort, which means partner of the monarch.

Speaking about the queen's dogs, she was given a corgi of her very own, called Susan, when she was eighteen.

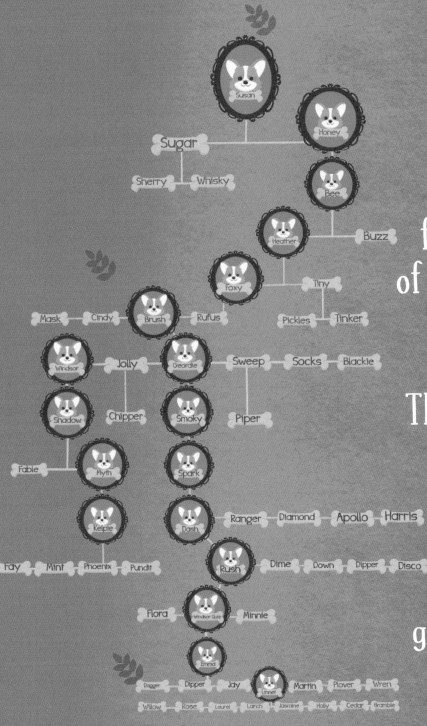

The queen had fourteen generations of Susan's descendants during her reign.

That means they were Susan's great-great- great-great- great- great-great-great- great- grandchildren!

She still has one of these dogs now, but it is a corgi crossed with a dachshund, because Princess Margaret, the queen's sister, liked dachshunds!

The queen is very busy, writing lots of letters, meeting people from all over the world

and sending postcards to people celebrating their golden and diamond anniversaries.

That means they have been married for fifty and sixty years.

She also sends postcards to those who are turning one hundred years old!

The queen and Prince Philip have celebrated their golden and diamond jubilees, but they are not yet 100 years old.

Philip is 99 years old and Queen Elizabeth is 94 years old!

Fun Facts about the Queen

- She's the longest reigning monarch in Britain

- Her favorite color is blue

- She has two birthdays: her actual birthday is April 21 but her official birthday is a Saturday in June when the weather is nicer

- Because British passports and drivers licenses are issued in her name, she doesn't need a passport to travel

- The Queen has sent out around 50,000 Christmas cards so far!

Printed in Great Britain
by Amazon